The Kissing Pot

Written by Linda Berg
Illustrated by Justin Flores

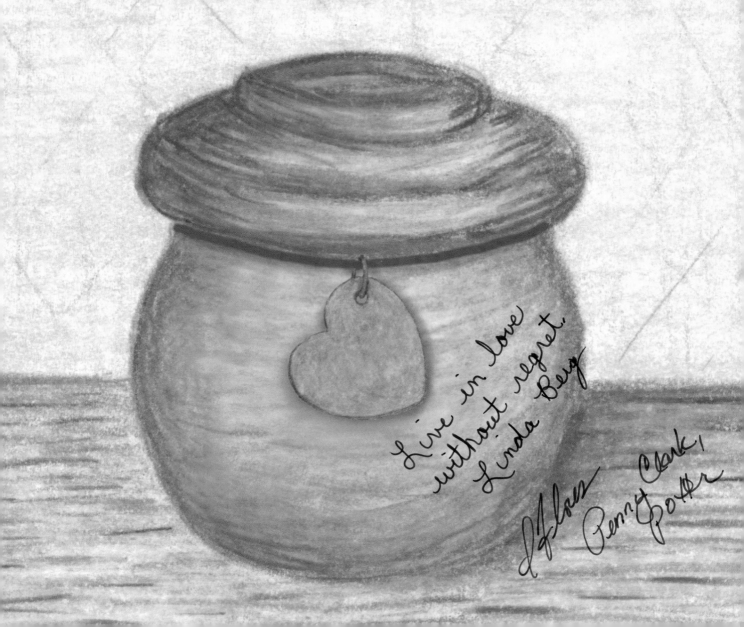

Live in love without regret.
Linda Berg

J Flores
Penny Clark,
Penny Potter

AuthorHouse™
1663 Liberty Drive
Bloomington, IN 47403
www.authorhouse.com
Phone: 1-800-839-8640

First published by AuthorHouse 5/17/2010

Printed in the United States of America
Bloomington, Indiana

This book is printed on acid-free paper.

This book is dedicated to Gene,
who gave me many wonderful gifts
in our short time together:
two beautiful daughters,
the best mother-in-law,
and the idea for this book.

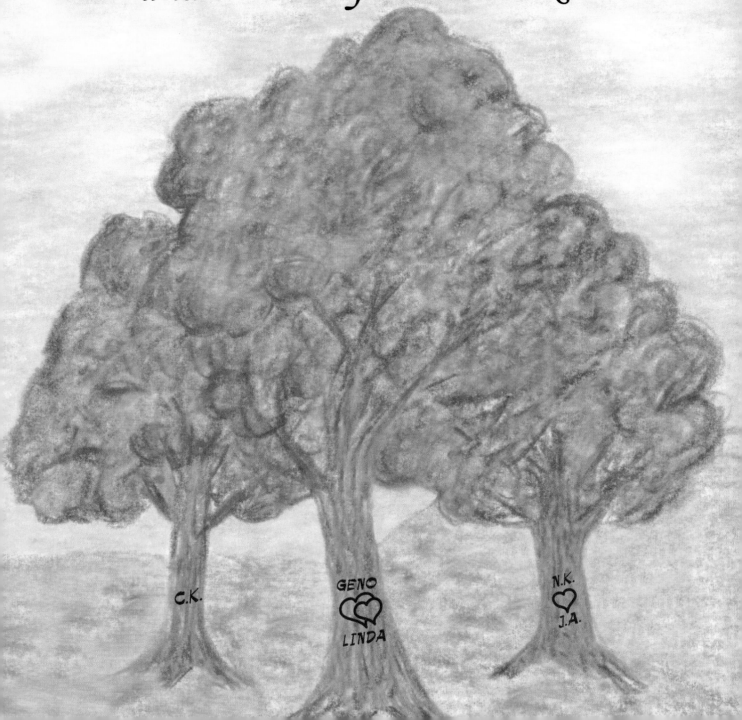

This book is presented to:

_____

Date: _____

Message: _____

_____

_____

_____

_____

_____

_____

From: _____

*Have you ever noticed
that two people
who truly love each other,
greet with a hug and a kiss?*

*They hug and kiss again
when they are going their
separate ways.*

*It might be because they are
unsure when they are going to be
together again.*

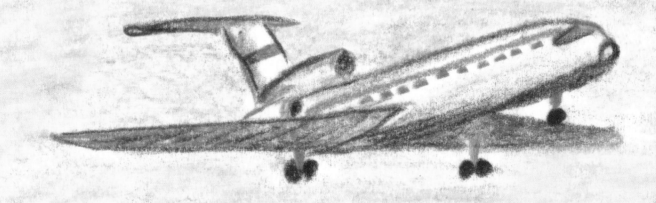

Every couple that gets married
makes a vow.
They promise to love and honor
each other.
Some even promise to obey.

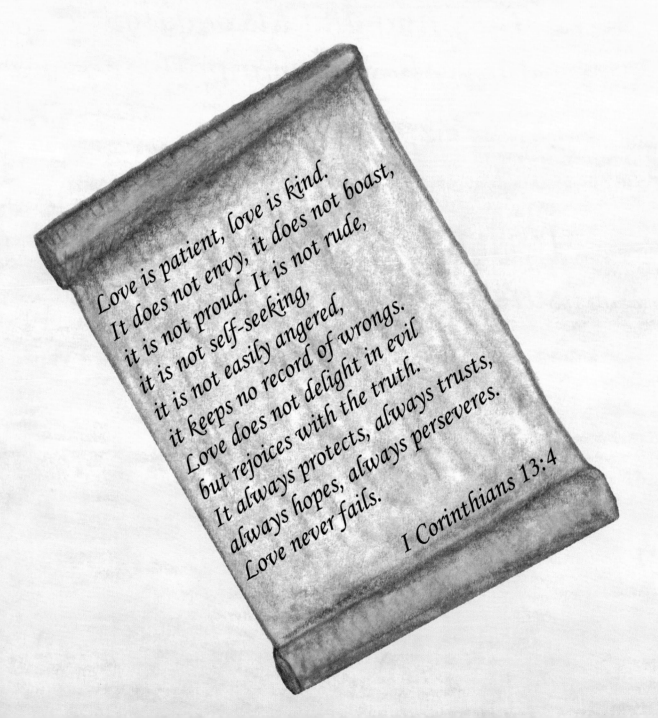

Love is patient, love is kind.
It does not envy, it does not boast,
it is not proud. It is not rude,
it is not self-seeking,
it is not easily angered,
it keeps no record of wrongs.
Love does not delight in evil
but rejoices with the truth.
It always protects, always trusts,
always hopes, always perseveres.
Love never fails.

I Corinthians 13:4

Some couples write

their own vows.

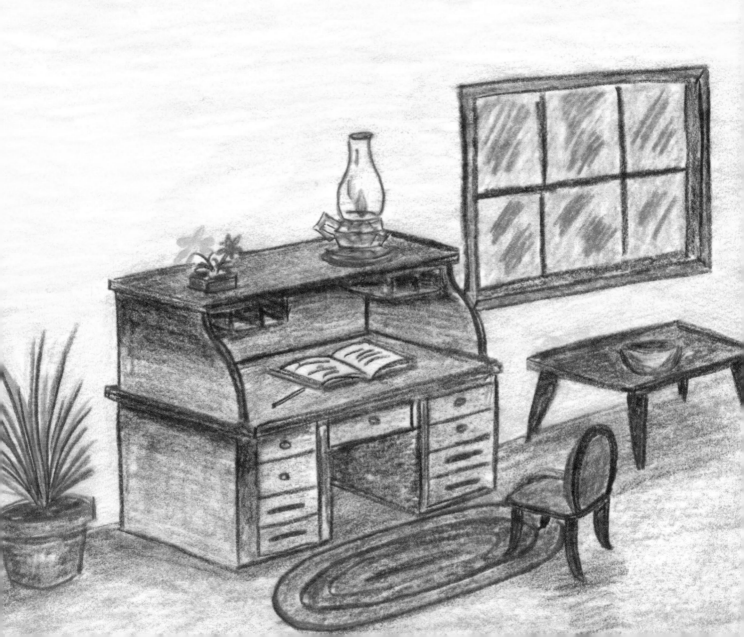

Usually couples will say these vows in front of the people at their wedding.

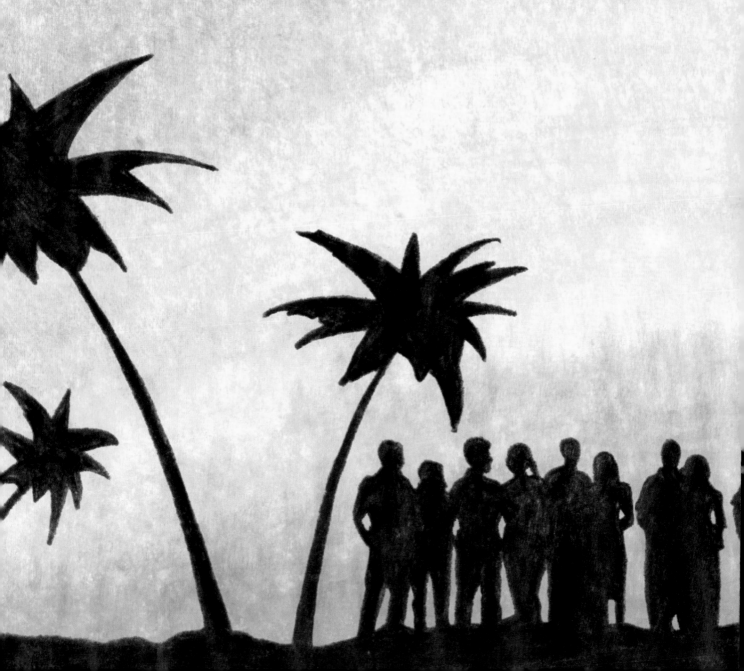

They often seal
this vow
with a kiss.

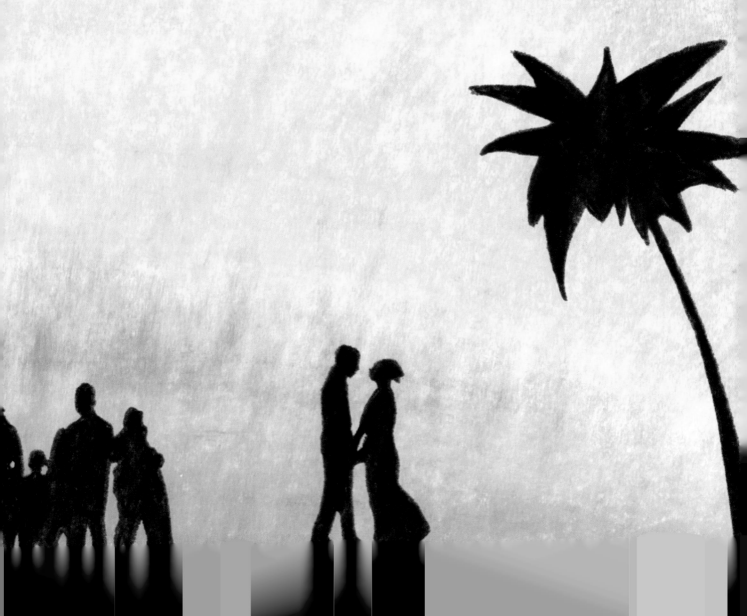

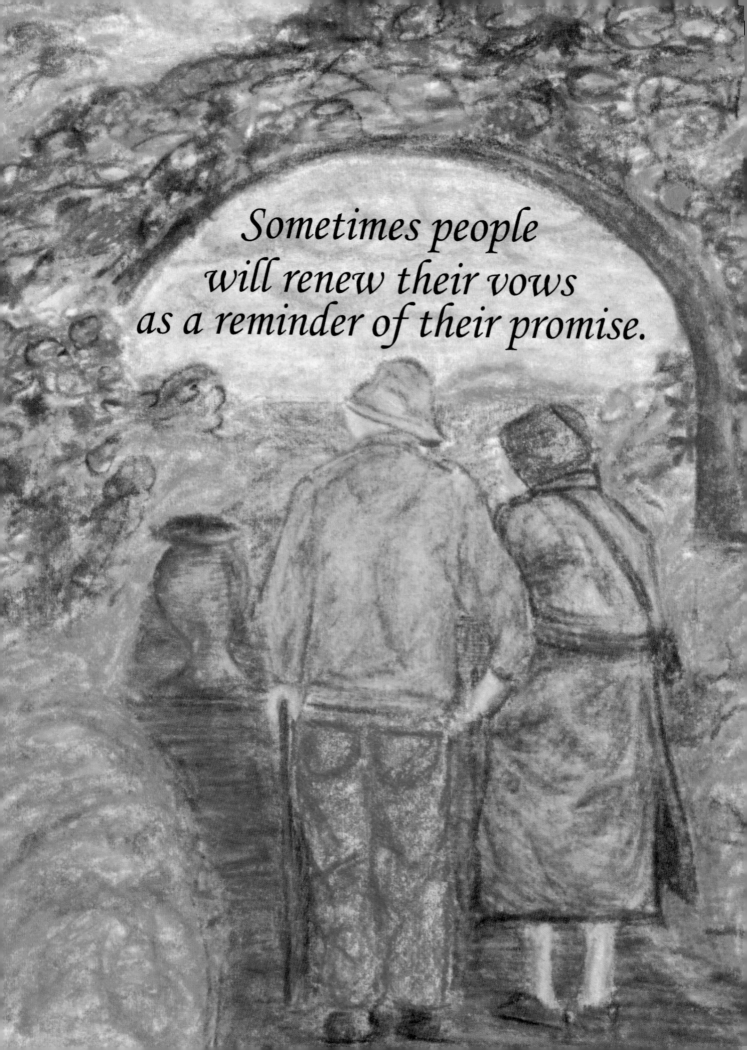

Sometimes people
will renew their vows
as a reminder of their promise.

As time passes, some people forget about their vows.

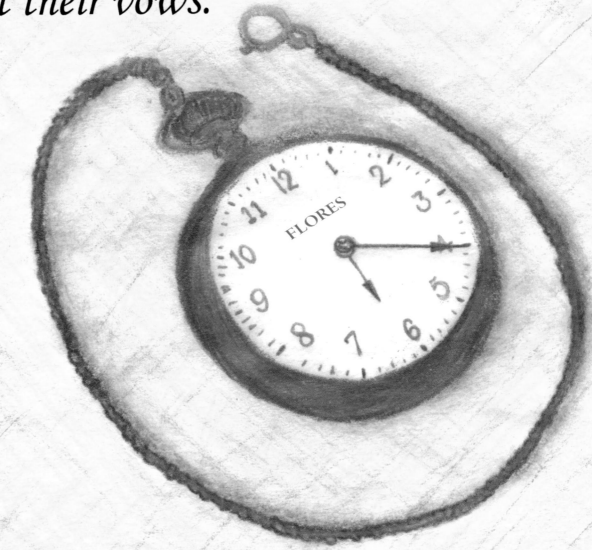

Some even forget to hug and kiss when they see each other or when they go their separate ways.

They start taking each other for granted - just assuming that the other person will always be there.

*Whenever you and your partner
go your separate ways, remember to
hug and kiss before you leave...*

and when you return.

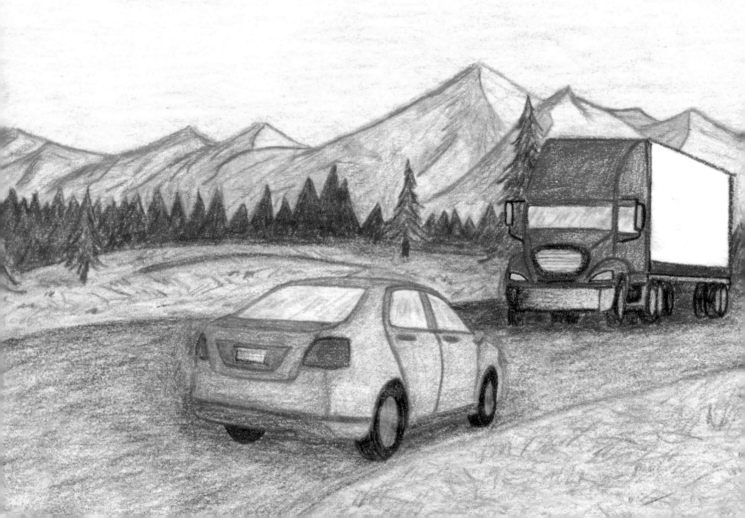

Here is a simple way to NOT take your love for granted.

If you forget to kiss your partner, you will owe a dollar or whatever amount the two of you decide upon.

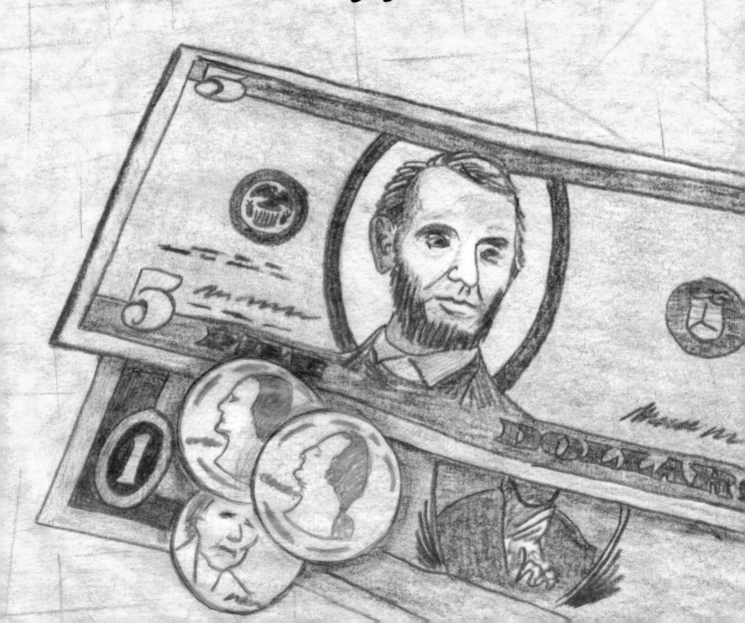

The amount gets placed
in The Kissing Pot.™
Now, there are rules about the
money in this pot.

NO ONE can borrow from it!!!

The money must be used together
and it's only for the two of you.

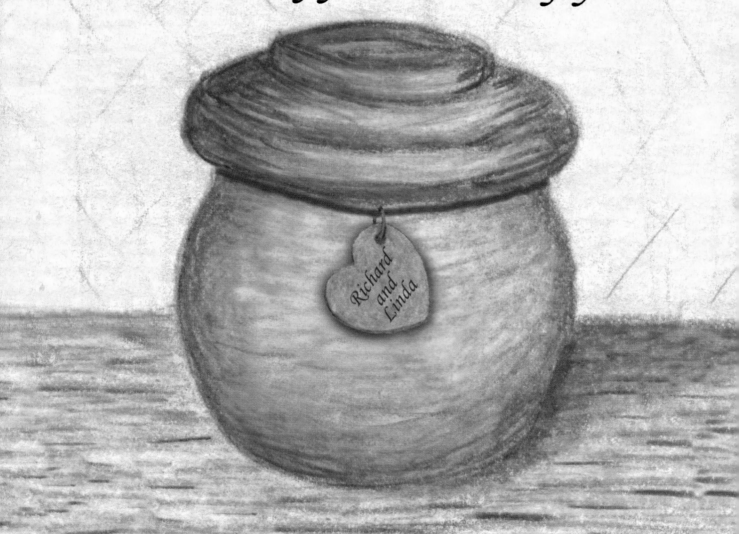

It is for going out for dinner...

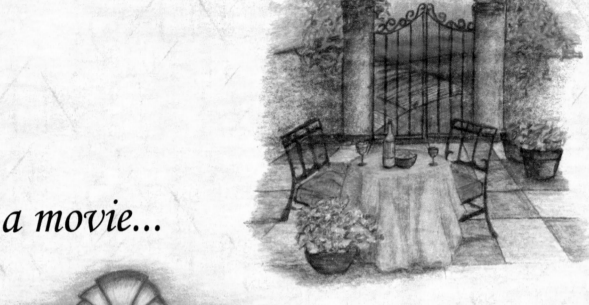

a movie...

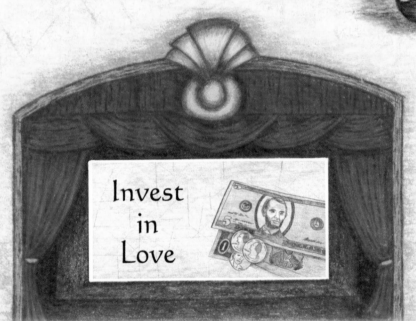

a romantic weekend...

or even a long vacation.

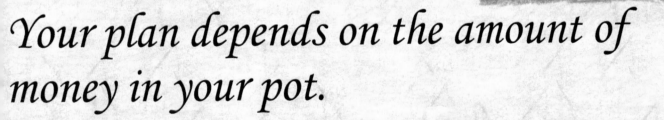

Your plan depends on the amount of money in your pot.

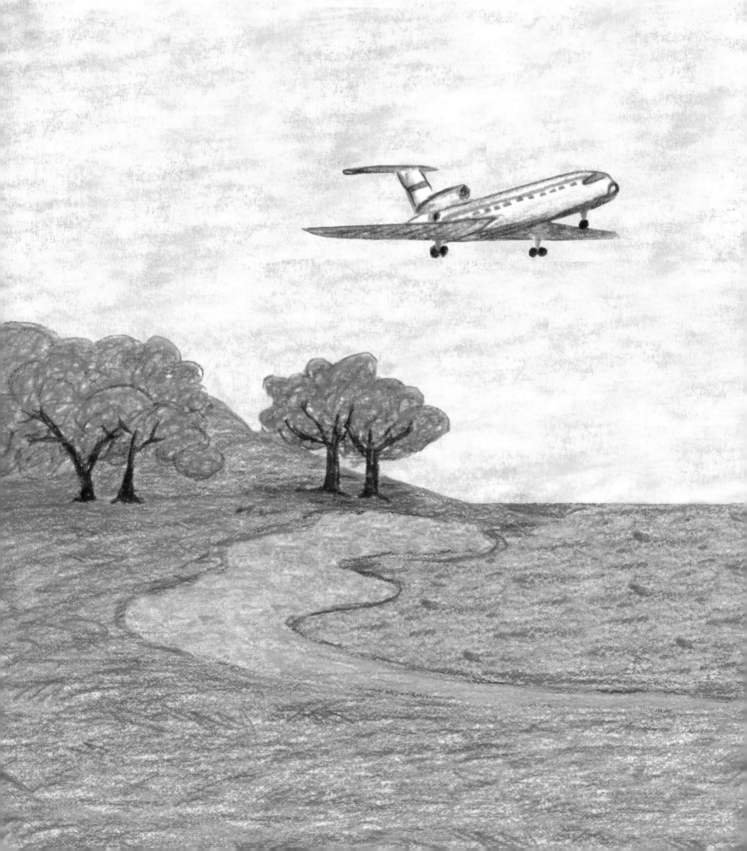

If you have enough money
for a long vacation...

you obviously
need to spend some time
with each other.

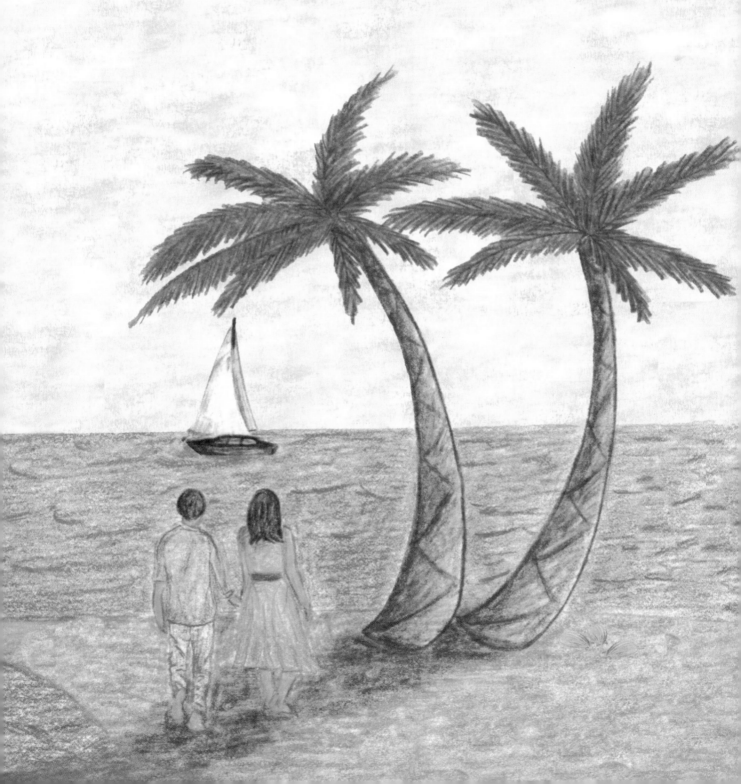

If you have enough money
for just a movie,
*that's a **good** thing.*

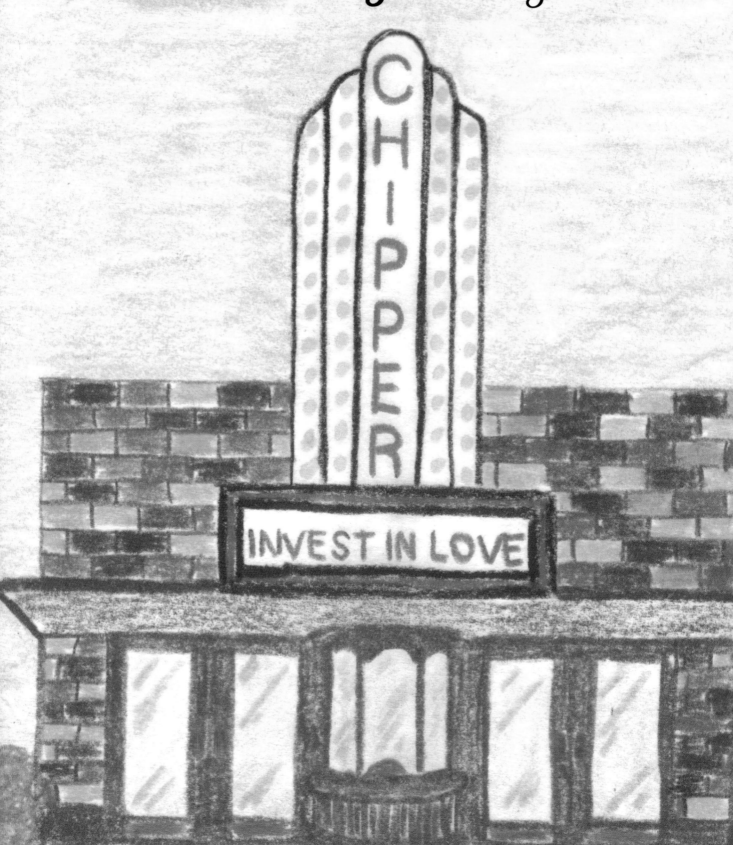

*Enough money
for renting a movie
is even better.*

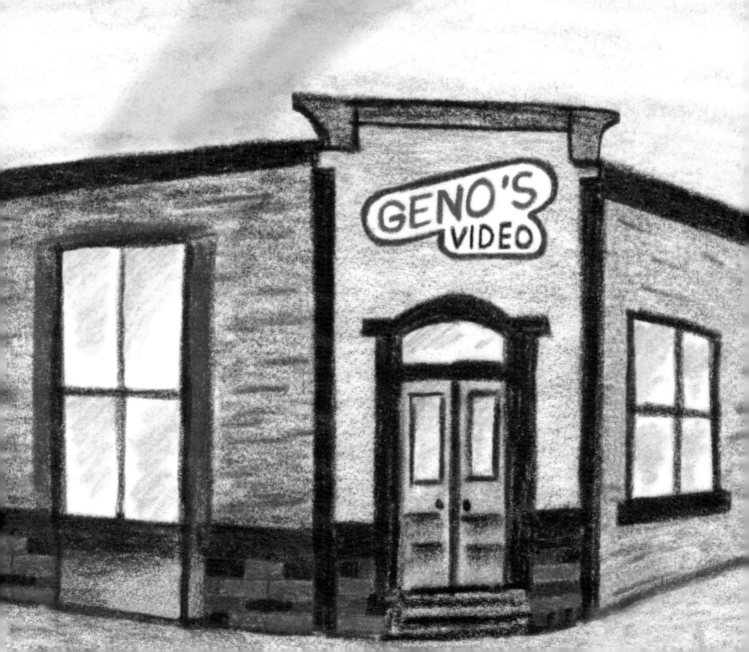

There was once a man who was going to hang out with the guys at the hunting shack.
He wanted to be sure that he didn't owe a buck when he returned.

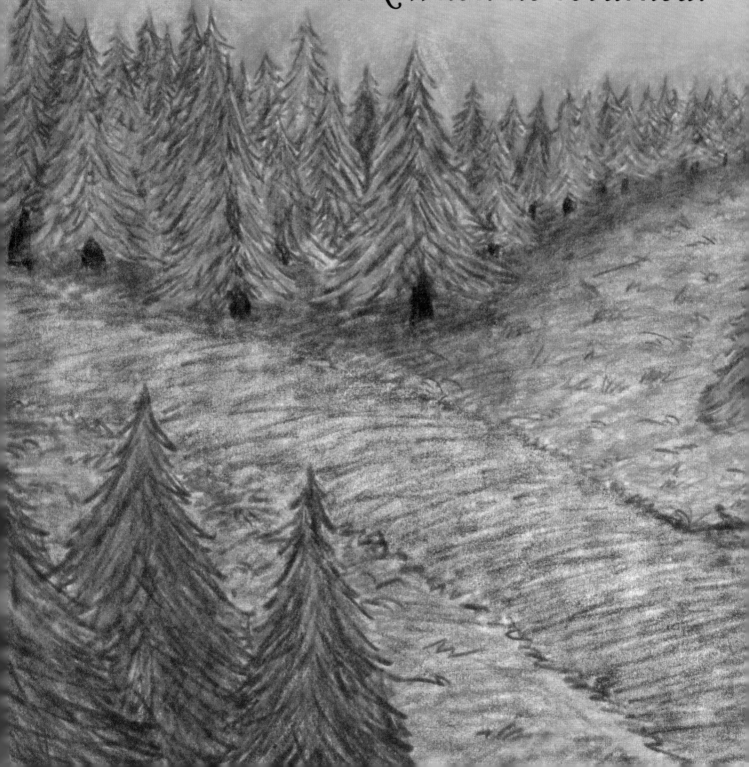

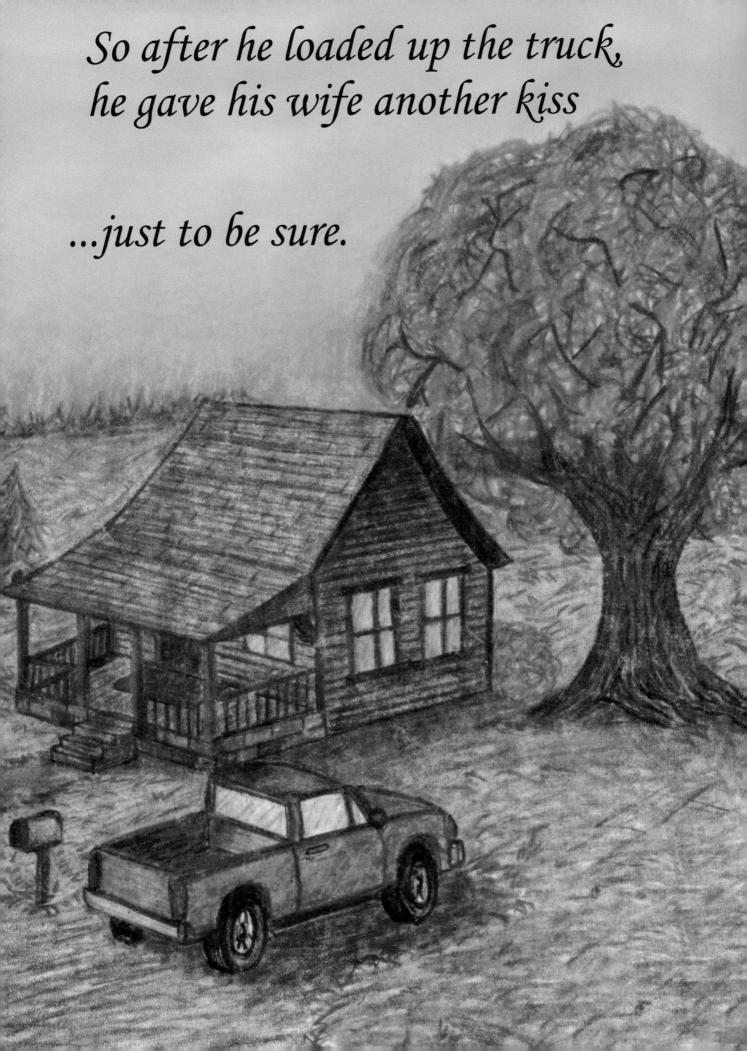

Little did he know,

he was leaving a legacy

for his family

and for you.

Don't take your partner for granted.

Remember to hug and kiss
your partner each time
that you separate and return.

And if you need to,
set your fine high
because - remember -
you can't take it with you
when you go!

So...

invest

in your love

now.

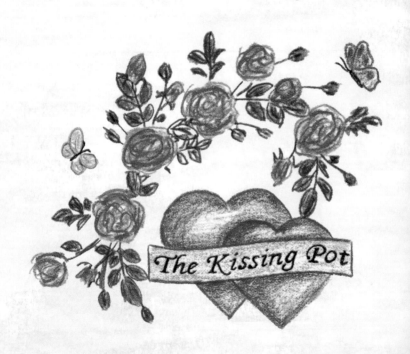

The Kissing Pot

Write your vows here:

_____
_____
_____
_____
_____
_____
_____
_____
_____
_____
_____
_____
_____

Fine for leaving or returning without a kiss:_____

Date:_____

Signatures:_____
_____

True love
Doesn't have
A happy ending...

Add photo of couple here.

Because true love
Doesn't end.

Growing Old Together

On these two pages add pictures of other couples that have influenced you such as parents and grandparents or add anniversary pictures.

The best is yet to come.